The Things We Bring with Us: Travel Poems

The Things We Bring with Us: Travel Poems

S.G. Huerta

Finalist for the Charlotte Mew Prize

HEADMISTRESS PRESS

Copyright © 2021 by S.G. Huerta
All rights reserved.

ISBN 978-1-7335345-7-4

This book may not be reproduced, in whole or in part, including illustrations, in any form (beyond that permitted by Sections 107 and 108 of the U.S. Copyright Law and except by reviewers for the public press), without written permission from the publishers.

Cover art © Katherine Bradford, Swim Team Outer Space (2015)
Cover & book design by Mary Meriam.

PUBLISHER
Headmistress Press
60 Shipview Lane
Sequim, WA 98382
Telephone: 917-428-8312
Email: headmistresspress@gmail.com
Website: headmistresspress.blogspot.com

for mom and dad

CONTENTS

The Things We Bring with Us	1
Sevilla	
La Virgen	3
In Santa Cruz	6
Plaza de España	8
Finding Lorca	9
Museo de Bellas Artes de Sevilla	11
New York	
On the Steps of St. Jean's	13
Posman Books at 30 Rock	14
LGA to DFW: Life Imitates Art	16
Italy	
Virgencita	18
Walking Through a Church in Spoleto	19
26 Piazza di Spagna	20
A Day in the Vatican	21
In Between	
Love Should Be Love	23
Back Home	
Mangled Pigeons	26
There's a Bodega in Lubbock	27
The Fish	28
We Didn't Cross the Border	30
About the Author	31
Acknowledgments	32

The Things We Bring with Us

White strangers often give me money
for traveling for work, for barely functioning
while gay and brown, for writing poems
about gayness and brownness. Never explicitly.
I accept the conditions, I mute my colors,
I shove every bright thing away into a suitcase,
fitting a lifetime into a carry-on. When told, I jump
at the chance to leave, to experience
marginalization elsewhere, to really have to take
my pills in case I lose my mind too far this time
from my sister's reach, to see if I can see
a future, a wife, a job
                              in another city,
a city with light and lighter baggage.

Sevilla

For one person who likes Spain there are a dozen who prefer books on her.
– Ernest Hemingway

La Virgen

"Just as abruptly as it started, the music stopped. The sound of an enchanting and motherly voice replaced it. A woman's voice was calling in Juan Diego's native Nahuatl language, 'Juantzin!'"
— Children's book found in a Chicana family's home

I spotted you in the Palacio,
Mother. You, brown-skinned,
who appeared to un Indio,
speaking in a tongue
foreign to the one
passed down to me
from my abuelita. My tongue,
I'm finding,
perfectly speaks
to our oppressors,
our history much shorter
than the pyramids
left by them to ruin,
left ruined by them,
our history beginning
at the Conquista.

Back in Corpus Christi,
Texas city named for the feast
all of Sevilla closes for,
my primas danced
folklórico, girls with thick brown hair
braided with red ribbons, boys

handsomely stamping their feet,
the nails attached to their black boots
making their presence known.
Here, the Sevillana dancer
expertly moves her skirt,
flashes of scarlet and black,
swishing in the style
I know from watching
Your children,
her horquilla falling
out of her hair
and onto the ground
from the *duende* of it all.
In this instance,
and many others
I've witnessed on this journey,
whose culture birthed whose?

I saw you, Mother,
cloaked in constellations,
on my walk – one of many –
to the Catedral, watching
over me and my classmates
and the street named for you.
In front of la Giralda,
three monjas pass me by,
habits white as the cigarettes
the old men in the bars
flick onto the street, and I consider
what could have been, what
could have not been – after all,

without La Niña would
my people even have
La Virgen?
My tongue,
I'm finding,
gets in the way
when I attempt to greet
the unassuming nuns
in my first language
with a telling outsider's dialect,
so I turn my attention
back up the looming
bell tower, and I am
as insignificant to the Giraldillo
at the top of it as a pigeon
at the foot of it.

In Santa Cruz

I look down at the map
that cost me five euros
and about twice as many
blisters on my feet
caused by my shitty
American sandals
on uneven sidewalks,
the door to the museum
hidden away between
cafes and storefronts.
A rough sketch of synagogues
of the past are highlighted
in white. *They are all churches
and restaurants now,* one
of the hundred Jews left in Sevilla
tells me in broken English.
I step through to the other side
of the curtain separating the single-room
exhibit.
      Is it even my place
to cry? What is it about this place?
A spiritualist raised Catholic, reduced
to tears, imposing myself
in the remains of the *Jewish Quarter,*
a lighter way to say ghetto,
or quarantine, barely able
to read about the atrocities

my family's church committed.

I try to exit through a small hall,
the walls covered in mirrors,
and I walk and walk.
I am facing ten of myself.

Plaza de España

Did you know they filmed *Star Wars* there? It was built in Sevilla in 1929. In 1929, my buelita was born in Villa de Santiago, México. El pueblo mágico. In 2018, I wandered through the Sevillana monument, too unsure of its present purpose to find a way inside. Alone. Too unsure to find a way out of my meditative trance until I hit a roadblock, a street performer, playing percussion, trash at first sight, drums on further inspection. Es una celebración de Iberoamérica, Spanish and Portuguese conquest of the Americas. Columbus set sail across the ocean blue on August 3, 1492. Less than 30 years later, the Aztec Empire fell. A lot happens in 30 years. Get married, have a baby, immigrate to the United States, leave behind el pueblo mágico. In the summer of 2018, I witnessed this celebration of Iberoamérica, crossed one of the bridges to get to the central fountain, escaping god knows what. God. The story says Moctezuma thought Cortés a god. It was too perfect, the serpent in the mouth of the eagle on the cactus. Something about perfect symmetry makes me uncomfortable. The perfect symmetry of the Spanish Square is no exception. The Spanish Square is not a square. Look at the fountains. I can't paint this picture for you. It's *Attack of the Clones*. They won't tell you it's the worst *Star Wars* movie, but I and god know better.

Finding Lorca

"Como no me he preocupado de nacer, no me preocupo de morir"
– Federico García Lorca in an interview two months before his death

I was nineteen,
finding that I could never love a man,
and looking up at a statue of one whose words
I could love. A man with a nineteen-year career–
stopped dead in its tracks– holding flowers
on his hundred and twentieth birthday,
a dulling but not yet dead pink bouquet shrouded
in greenery that somebody must have placed
between his outstretched bronze arms
and the outstretched wings of the bronze bird
in his hands. A red rendering of Velázquez's meninas
waits a few yards behind him.
"Madrid a Federico García Lorca" reads the inscription
with a penciled-in tilde.
                          He wasn't worried to be born,
he wasn't worried about death, but looking up at him,
and living where he died, I can't help but fear,
perhaps irrationally, I will have the same end.
In Granada, I climbed to the top of a mirador
with another poet for a view of the Alhambra,
a sight Lorca surely knew well
before his execution. We argued
about what ravine may be your resting place.
The place doesn't matter.
Atop this hill, looking out

onto the top of another,
I become that bronze bird.

June 2018

Museo de Bellas Artes de Sevilla

I challenged myself to identify
the pantheon of "big S" Saints
and Catholic figures depicted
before reading the descriptions
stuck to the wall, a nostalgic game.
There's St. Francis, holding an infant Jesus.
No skulls in sight. Is that chronologically
correct? Here, Justa and Rufina
present a detached Giralda.
That would make a nice bookmark.
In another hall, David, with a look
of intense worry – guilt? – drags
Goliath's head behind him.
A glass case protects the head of John
the Baptist from further mutilation.
His half-closed eyes follow me
around the room as I continue
to test my status of recovering Catholic.
I have five Euro in my pocket.
Which print should I buy
and memorialize? Who can accompany
la Virgen de Guadalupe on my wall
in West Texas? St. Francis is back,
at the site of the crucifixion,
and in the corner of the oil painting: a skull.

New York

New York is something awful, something monstrous. I like to walk the streets, lost, but I recognize that New York is the world's greatest lie.
– Federico García Lorca

On the Steps of St. Jean's

And although this half empty New York City
cathedral boasts high ceilings,

high enough to house the city's
pigeons, I suffocated under

the woman I made love to last week,
claustrophobic in that cliché closet

barely containing me or my pantheon of sins.
The man of God at the lectern turned

my stomach, added on to my cab sickness –
buy these books for $24.95 each, he says,

and maybe *you'll be healed* –
I'm outside, praying to Mary through

heaving breaths, developing a contact
high from the cloud of smoke from around

the corner. Her Son and his mouthpiece are too
intimidating, so I seek the comfort of a woman instead.

Posman Books at 30 Rock
After Eileen Myles

How do you write
an Eileen Myles poem
with only half
their confidence,
all their privacy,
twice their lesbian
loneliness?
Short lines,
rich metaphors
for imperfect love,
more Kerouac
than Kerouac,
minus
the fabricated
authenticity.
Do you write
a story
about wandering into
the concourse
at 30 Rockefeller,
brushing hands
with the cashier?
She says,
"follow me,
I curated this
poetry section,"
and you buy *Not Me*

with her discount.
You think
you had a moment
with her,
two displaced
Texans
who left to find
community –
do you write
at the end
that she never
answers your email?

LGA to DFW: Life Imitates Art

Outside the window of an aircraft,
the sky is a Georgia O'Keeffe painting,
thin pink brush strokes above fluff
of white clouds above too blue sky,
unattainable from behind the prison of glass.

Italy

Awake for ever in a sweet unrest...
– John Keats

Virgencita

My mother tells me to speak Spanish
if I trip up on my limited Italian.
I'm dressed in guilt for a trip I have
yet to take, guilt for the Easter
clothes hanging up unworn;
the blue floral dress and I

have traded places.
Limited research tells me
I could sleep with a woman,
marry her, were I Italian.
Pope Francis says he shouldn't judge,
but my marriage?
                Godless.
There could be room for Mary.

Walking Through a Church in Spoleto

Bells chimed
as I read the placard detailing
the church's rules. I broke
them all: pink tank top, washed out
denim shorts, desecrated temple
of a body. I can't read Italian,
don't know how to pray here,
or anywhere.
Captured in a panoramic photo:
Our disembodied limbs, distorted faces,
that even a Mother could love.

26 Piazza di Spagna

John Keats' deathbed over-
and underwhelmed me.
He didn't sleep or die there.
The Pope ordered the original bed to burn
to stop the spread of tuberculosis.
Keats and his fears of ceasing to be…
Walking around his room
with my dad, neither of us coughed up
blood. I ignored the signage –
fucking tourist – and touched
the comforter. It was green.
I turned to my father, expecting a scolding –
where did he go?
                    Back downstairs?
I circled the tiny room again, blinded
myself making sure the sun still shone
outside the small window. Love,
to nothingness, does sink.

A Day in the Vatican

You inherit nothing from your father
apart from Catholicism and bipolar.
You ditch the former and smoke
the latter out.

Meet where it began, formally,
the first Holy Father buried below
the Basilica's altar, footsteps falling
with your father's,

following his path into the side chapel
to say a quick Hail Mary or two,
his path to alcoholism that reveals
itself upon leaving

the Basilica, approaching a vendor,
buying two beers, downing them both
while greeting two nuns. *Dangerously close,*
Chad Davidson writes,

as if there were another kind of nearness.
The nuns respond in English, the beers
a normality, expected for the duo standing
a foot apart, one smiling.

In Between

Listen, I have been educated.
I have learned about Western
Civilization. Do you know
What the message of Western
Civilization is? I am alone.
　　　　　　– Eileen Myles, "An American Poem"

Love Should Be Love

There is a coffee shop
        in Roswell,
New Mexico,
        where we stopped
along the way
        to Santa Fe,
recommended by Karina,
        where I bought
your iced latte,
        and later
a postcard for your
        little sister,
because I so desperately
        need her approval
and yours.
        You felt safe
enough to hold
        my hand
in yours,
        icy,
in that UFO museum,
        rows and rows
of doctored photos,
        fakes, *phonies*.
What if we could
        stay in
that postcard,

                happy family
        of aliens, not standing out
                in Roswell
        or anywhere? Not break-
                ing back home.

Back Home

Living in literature and love is the best thing there is. You're always home.
  – Eileen Myles

Mangled Pigeons

My first Sunday
back home from Spain,
or back to West Texas, at least,
I saw a disembodied,
                        bloody,
pigeon head by my mailbox.
I always joked that I'd title
a collection of poems
about Lubbock
Mangled Pigeons
(and Other Poems).

I left my red Converse
in Spain; my toes were sticking out–
my disorder returned
with me, though bipolar, never leaving.
It carefully tucked itself into
the worn insoles of my shoes
I brought back,
and TSA did not catch on.

The whites of my new red Converse shine
too brightly; the red is artificial,
                            unnatural,
especially when compared
to that pigeon head by my mailbox.

There's a Bodega in Lubbock

I wouldn't call it that, but who am I
to disagree with green neon letters,
West Texas authority. The decal
on the tinted window reads,
"A grocery store in an urban area."
A piece of NYC right down the street.
I pick up American Spirits and canned
wine at least three times a week,
talk to the English major behind the counter,
pretend this ritual replaces personality.
Imagine a New Yorker in Lubbock,
expecting a bagel at the bodega
but getting tacos y $1 cerveza instead.
Imagine a gutsy Lubbock pigeon in New York,
wanting to befriend everyone when everyone
keeps walking on. Imagine how slowly
she would walk compared to the others,
how slowly she would take flight upon
being approached–
Imagine a New Yorker in the bodega
down the street, but all they find
for lunch is two English majors
and a pigeon.

The fish

rather, crawfish, rescued
from a fourth grade classroom, gently retanked
in mom's kitchen. Between

plastic plants and fake rocks,
my new pet lay motionless for three days–
Maybe he's just molting.

He was not molting. No,
after a weekend at dad's bachelor pad,
the crawfish, still, unmoved.

Did I feed him expired
fish flakes? Did he eat them? Was there too much
love? Did I make him leave?

We held a funeral,
mom, my brother, and I, but my sister
refused to attend it.

My sister never left
the old house on Rainier to see our dad
or the new apartment.

I envy her choices,
her shield from pain, crawfish-
or father-related.

We never spoke of him
again after watching him leave, swiftly,
gone for good down the drain.

We Didn't Cross the Border

I'm imagining a place I've never been, and a city
in Nuevo León I visited once as a child where
my primos spoke English and my mother spoke
Spanish. I don't want to spit in a tube, outline exactly
how colonialism shaped me, my lighter but
not light skin, dark eyes, darker hair. Manic
depression and instability run through my veins.
My father, mexicoamericano born in England,
had no roots. ¿Su necesidad? ¿voluntad? By 20,
I'd moved, at minimum, thirteen times. I flourish
in transit, never tied to Dallas skyscrapers and the bustling
downtown my dad used to patrol, nor to the empty
skies in Lubbock pressing down on me. Nothing
flourishes on the paternal family land in Concepción,
south of Kingsville, no crops take root unless you
count the nopal en el frente. Pre-1836, the land
was likely as useless as it is now: un burro named Jack
who won't bray, thirty goats whose eyes glow
at night, the promise — threat — of an anglicized
Llorona despite Kingsville's distance from la agua…
Esta no es poema. This is autoetnografía.
My father was a runner in high school —
we haven't stopped.

ABOUT THE AUTHOR

S. G. Huerta is a Chicana poet from Dallas, Texas. They are currently pursuing their MFA at Texas State University and they live in Texas with their cat, Lorca. Find them on Twitter @ sg_poetry.

ACKNOWLEDGMENTS

Harbinger: "In Santa Cruz"

Thank you to Julian Banuelos, Karina Ocañas, Sara Ryan, Hali Cardenas, John Poch, Diandra Osorio, and my family for believing in these poems as well as my queer chicana self.

HEADMISTRESS PRESS BOOKS

Demoted Planet - Katherine Fallon
Earlier Households - Bonnie J. Morris
The Things We Bring with Us: Travel Poems - S.G. Huerta
The Water Between Us - Gillian Ebersole
Discomfort - Sarah Caulfield
The History of a Voice - Jessica Jopp
I Wish My Father - Lesléa Newman
Tender Age - Luiza Flynn-Goodlett
Low-water's Edge - Jean A. Kingsley
Routine Bloodwork - Colleen McKee
Queer Hagiographies - Audra Puchalski
Why I Never Finished My Dissertation - Laura Foley
The Princess of Pain - Carolyn Gage & Sudie Rakusin
Seed - Janice Gould
Riding with Anne Sexton - Jen Rouse
Spoiled Meat - Nicole Santalucia
Cake - Jen Rouse
The Salt and the Song - Virginia Petrucci
mad girl's crush tweet - summer jade leavitt
Saturn coming out of its Retrograde - Briana Roldan
i am this girl - gina marie bernard
Week/End - Sarah Duncan
My Girl's Green Jacket - Mary Meriam
Nuts in Nutland - Mary Meriam & Hannah Barrett
Lovely - Lesléa Newman
Teeth & Teeth - Robin Reagler
How Distant the City - Freesia McKee
Shopgirls - Marissa Higgins
Riddle - Diane Fortney
When She Woke She Was an Open Field - Hilary Brown

A Crown of Violets - Renée Vivien tr. Samantha Pious
Fireworks in the Graveyard - Joy Ladin
Social Dance - Carolyn Boll
The Force of Gratitude - Janice Gould
Spine - Sarah Caulfield
I Wore the Only Garden I've Ever Grown - Kathryn Leland
Diatribe from the Library - Farrell Greenwald Brenner
Blind Girl Grunt - Constance Merritt
Acid and Tender - Jen Rouse
Beautiful Machinery - Wendy DeGroat
Odd Mercy - Gail Thomas
The Great Scissor Hunt - Jessica K. Hylton
A Bracelet of Honeybees - Lynn Strongin
Whirlwind @ Lesbos - Risa Denenberg
The Body's Alphabet - Ann Tweedy
First name Barbie last name Doll - Maureen Bocka
Heaven to Me - Abe Louise Young
Sticky - Carter Steinmann
Tiger Laughs When You Push - Ruth Lehrer
Night Ringing - Laura Foley
Paper Cranes - Dinah Dietrich
On Loving a Saudi Girl - Carina Yun
The Burn Poems - Lynn Strongin
I Carry My Mother - Lesléa Newman
Distant Music - Joan Annsfire
The Awful Suicidal Swans - Flower Conroy
Joy Street - Laura Foley
Chiaroscuro Kisses - G.L. Morrison
The Lillian Trilogy - Mary Meriam
Lady of the Moon - Amy Lowell, Lillian Faderman, Mary Meriam
Irresistible Sonnets - ed. Mary Meriam
Lavender Review - ed. Mary Meriam

www.ingramcontent.com/pod-product-compliance
Lightning Source LLC
Chambersburg PA
CBHW060223050426
42446CB00013B/3154